P9-AFN-517

To
Gretchen —
May you continue
Reaching others,
self and your
own special
goals!
Connie Hunt
6/4/81

R
E
A
C
H
I
N
G

by

Connie Hunt

Pulsar ─☼─ Publications

P~ULSAR~ —☼— P~UBLICATIONS~

Box 714
Lafayette, CA
94549

Reaching
toward
Wholeness

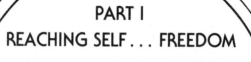

PART I
REACHING SELF . . . FREEDOM

PART II
REACHING OTHERS . . . . LOVE

PART III
REACHING GOD . . . . . . TRUTH

PART I

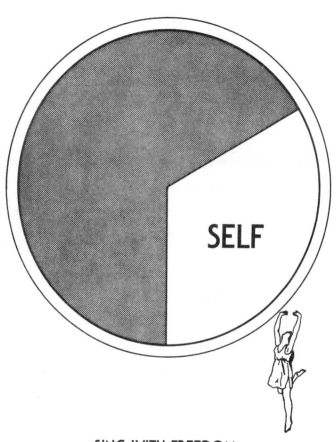

SING WITH FREEDOM

AND CELEBRATE

YOURSELF

THE SEARCH

And so, I was born . . .
A creature quite unique,
Who could reason, think
Remember, even speak.

I sat down to ponder
What my life was all about.
If I could think and reason
Surely I could find that out?

Years went by and I grew and grew
Taller in stature,
But smaller too.
As my knowledge of the world
Increased in size
My own narrow world was minimized.

How could I so confined
Know my destiny?
Surely there was meant
Some prominence for me.

To find a love,
A passion to be true,
Seemed the least of what
I was meant to do.

But how to find this love
And how to know real passion?
I could seek wisdom from above
Or from prevailing fashion . . .

Or I could gaze within my soul,
And find my own unblemished goal.
For as I saw more clearly
The plan divine,
I knew the universal soul
Was one with mine.

UPWARD MOBILITY

TO REACH THE TOP
OH HOW WE STRIVE
WITHOUT KNOWING WHICH
WAY IS "UP"
OR WHEN WE HAVE ARRIVED.

LIFE'S WORK

Work is too often seen as duty
that binds our souls to earth
rather than a source of beauty
giving individuals worth.

To seek to know ourselves
through our creative life
is work enough
without the added strife

of the world's desire
to quench creative fire
keep mankind at the plow.
Rise up creators and
seek your birthright now.

The right to be, to think, to wonder
must never be plowed asunder.
Labor, if chosen by each one,
will be rewarding and well done.

To accept each one's choice we must
have faith in human kind
and through this act of trust
will be born our peace of mind.

CHANGE

I MUST KEEP MY LIFE

WRITTEN IN PENCIL

SO I CAN ERASE AND CHANGE IT.

SYMBIOSIS

ANGER IS A HEALTHY SIGN
OF DIFFERENCE
IN YOUR VIEW AND MINE.

CONFLICT IS THE CUTTING EDGE
OF CHANGES
THAT WE OFTEN DREAD.

WHY ARE ANGER – – CONFLICT
WORDS OF SCORN?
WHEN FROM THEM
CHOICE AND CHANGE
ARE BORN?

POTENTIAL

I'M HAUNTED BY WHAT I COULD BE

IMPRISONED BY WHAT I SHOULD BE

SET FREE BY WHAT I WOULD BE.

THE BOX

LET ME OUT!
I DON'T WANT TO FIT
INTO YOUR BOX.

MY SOUL MUST HAVE
ROOM TO GROW.

NOT JUST TO THE BORDERS
OF YOUR MIND,
BUT TO THE LIMITS OF
MY OWN VISION.

OH, DO NOT TRY TO
MAKE ME SMALL,
BECAUSE YOUR OWN
WORLD IS SO NARROW.

I MUST BE FREE
TO EXPRESS
THE EVER-CHANGING ME.

IF YOU MUST BE BOUND
TO FEEL SECURE,
I MUST FEEL BOUNDLESS
TO ENDURE.

PUSHING EVER OUTWARD . . .
MY WORLD GROWS LARGER
AND I GROW WITH IT
TOWARD MY DESTINY.

AUTHOR'S NOTE

This poem was conceived one morning while preparing breakfast. I was mulling over how to tell a friend that I couldn't help her with a special project, when a phrase from an assertiveness class popped into my head: "You're not saying no to all these worthy causes, you're saying yes to yourself."

That thought kept me going for months, but one day I realized that sometimes it was right to say yes, and wrote the poem on the next page.

LIFE IS REALLY A BALANCE.

SAYING NO

In the course of my life
I've been forced to say no
In every conceivable way.
NO, I'm busy, I'm out of touch.

No, I couldn't help you that much
I've gone back to school you see
To seek what I was meant to be.

I've taken a job
working six hours a day,
How could I possibly
Plan that luncheon in May?

I've children to drive
And a husband to feed.
Surely you can find
Someone else more in need
Of helping the church..
Community, scouts...

I'm finding myself,
Which leaves me out.

Oh, it has been a trying time
Fighting other's demands
Myself to find.

But if my NO causes distress
Please remember....
I'm not saying no to you
But to myself YES!

OUR LIVES MIRROR OUR BELIEFS

SAYING YES

In the course of my life
I have often said yes
with a resigned sigh.

Saying yes, you see, usually
implicates me in something
I wouldn't normally try.

But I must say this
that without some risk
I would never be
who I am today.

For each "yes" brought me
an opportunity
to view life in a new way.

Though at times, a straight "no"
can save vertigo,
I have been most blest
by the times I've said "yes".

HOPE IS INSTINCTIVE
DESPAIR IS LEARNED.

THE TREE OF LIFE

As we climb the tree of life
We follow one branch after another
Seeking peace, running from strife
Trying to discern one from the other.

We wait for the buds of life to bloom
And hold fast as the winds blow,
But the Fall rushes in much too soon
And the flowers often do not grow.

Don't wait, cry the leaves
As the wind rushes through.
Don't wait for the flowers to bloom.
Keep climbing up the tree,
To yourself be true,
Don't wait in the shade of gloom.

Grow right to the top
Where the sunbeams shine
Where all is light and energy.
Keep growing up into the air divine
Where one can be truly free.

MATURITY

MATURITY IS BEING AWARE

OF THE WORLD AS IT IS

WITHOUT EVER LOOSING SIGHT OF

WHAT IT MIGHT BE.

THE NEW "ISM"

PATHOS AND PAIN
CAN BE QUITE A STRAIN
ON TRUE IDEALISM.

HOW CAN WE COPE
WITHOUT ANY HOPE
EXPRESSED BY SUCH REALISM?

WHY WOULD WE WANT TO LIVE
UNLESS WE COULD GIVE
A LITTLE OPTIMISM?

IF ALL IS LOST
TOO GREAT'S THE COST
OF THE CURRENT HUMANISM.

SOMEDAY...
WHEN I FIND THE TIME
I'LL SIT AWHILE AND WRITE A LINE.
I'LL TAKE A WALK AND SEE A FRIEND
ENJOY THE DAY FROM END TO END.

BUT WHAT IF "SOMEDAY"
NEVER COMES?

MORE OR LESS

I want more

love. . . more feeling

I need less. . .

objects. . . for stealing

More life based on an ideal

Less views I feel I must conceal

Less time spent in mundane zeal

That makes my life seem so unreal

More time in which to reveal

All the things I truly feel.

EVERYONE IS ALWAYS

SEEKING MEANING

WITHOUT REALIZING

THEY MUST SUPPLY IT.

FATE

What are you fate?
What decree defines you?
Are you a trait
or reasoned rendevous?

How can I face you
knowing not whether
you are destined
or a goal I've sought?

Must you haunt me every day?
Must I listen to what you say?

If only I could shift
your twisted sway
and live my life
in my own way.

But how to change
the skein of time
and make my life
completely mine?

FREEDOM OF EXPRESSION

A thought was born
seeking expression.

Fenced in by rules and beliefs
it rose to the realm of fantasy
where it would be free to create
new thoughts within a circle of
acceptance
safe from the "real" world.

For the people in fantasy land
are not bound by the "way it is"
but open to the way it could be.

AUTHOR'S NOTE

While on an all night cruise of the Bay with my daughter's graduation class, I began to wonder about the way we divide time and segment our lives. Staying up all night, time seemed more like a continuous river flowing on endlessly, and life a series of "Graduations."

GRADUATION

LIFE UNFURLS A RIBBONED LENGTH

OF TIME

WITH IMAGES STATUED ON THE MIND.

CONTINUOUS

GRADUATIONS

CAP AND GOWN OUR DAYS

AS NEW INSIGHTS REPLACE OLD WAYS

OF EXPERIENCING LIFE

ITS LENGTH AND BREADTH.

WHAT TRUTHS

WILL STAND

UNDAUNTED

AT

OUR

DEATH?

DREAM ON. . .

FOR DREAMS ARE ONLY LIFE

WE HAVE YET TO EXPERIENCE.

PART II

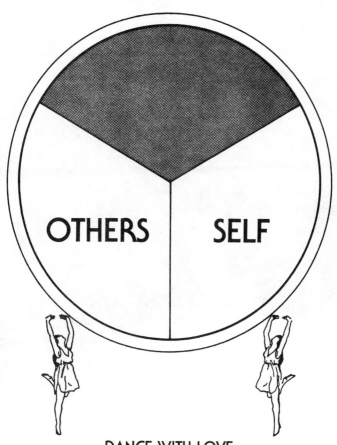

OTHERS | SELF

DANCE WITH LOVE

AND CELEBRATE

OTHERS

AUTHOR'S NOTE

The first time I met Maya Angelou, the poet, I was struck by her sense of inner knowing. It was a great high for me tinged with deep sadness that we as human beings are missing so much in the relationship we could have to one another. I wrote this poem for her and us.

YOU'VE TOUCHED ME

Your life has touched me.
The sight of you
The sound of your voice
Bring waves of precognition
Making me rejoice.

Some identity at the core of my being
Responds to your presence
As though I am seeing myself
With no pretense.

I feel a common bond of mortality
Running deep and wide.
With a great will of effort
I keep the tears inside.

I mustn't let the whole world see
How deeply you have touched me,
For that would set my longing free
And I would cry for humanity.

TRANSISTION

I feel as barren as a winter tree

Bereft of friends and family

Left only with the memory of what

Our life together used to be.

As we seek our own opportunity

I ask: "Have I left them or

Have they left me?"

MEMORIES

Nothing is ever the same
Each encounter is precious, unique.
My heart is filled with pain
To think of shared moments so sweet.

How poignant to know
They have ended.
How consoling to know
They can't change.

All our shared moments
Are suspended
In our memories
Where they cannot change.

FENCES DO NOT KEEP ENEMIES WITHOUT,

THEY KEEP PRISONERS WITHIN.

WHO WILL LISTEN

HEAR ME . . . HEAR ME

THE WHOLE WORLD CRIES

BUT WHO WILL LISTEN?

HEAR <u>ME</u> . . . HEAR <u>ME</u>

WE ALL CRY

BUT WILL WE LISTEN?

LOVE ME . . . LOVE ME

THE WHOLE WORLD CRIES

BUT WHO WILL CARE?

LOVE <u>ME</u> . . . LOVE <u>ME</u>

WE ALL CRY

BUT WILL WE CARE?

REALITY . . . REALITY

YOURS EXPLAINS YOU

MINE EXPLAINS ME

IF ONLY WE COULD EXPLAIN

EACH OTHER TO ONE ANOTHER

WHAT A DIFFERENT WORLD THIS

WOULD BE.

ACCEPTANCE

ACCEPTANCE IS A SIMPLE WORD
WHOSE DEFINITION WE'VE ALL HEARD

AND YET A SIMPLE WORD
IS NOT A SIMPLE DEED,
LOVE IN ACTION NOT IN THEORY
IS WHAT WE NEED.

ACCEPTANCE COULD BE THE SEED
OF A NEW AGE,
WHERE OLD DISSENSIONS END
AND WE ALL DISCOVER
EACH OTHER AS FRIEND.

OUR LIVES ARE UNFOLDING

AS WE STRUGGLE DAY BY DAY

TO SEE OURSELVES ANEW

TURN OLD BELIEFS AWAY.

BELIEVING

The magic of believing
In everything you do
Is the magic of achieving
And making dreams come true.

If you believe you're special
(Really quite unique)
You <u>will</u> be special, for
You are what you think.

Beliefs are part of all of us
Creating our life style.
Your beliefs will determine if
You greet life with a smile.

So take a look at all your limits
And review your guiding rules.
Your beliefs may be preventing growth
By the narrowness of your views.

IT'S HOW YOU HANDLE

YOUR JOY AND YOUR SORROW

FOR WHAT YOU DO TODAY

WILL DETERMINE YOUR TOMORROW..

REUNIONS

How temporal our touching
How tempting to tears
Remembering the passing
Of all those years.

We gather together
Not expressing our fears
Of losing each other
Over the years.

FORGIVENESS

I could forgive you

But if I do

I must make assumptions

And be the judge of you.

And judging is a wasteful game

When we are really just the same.

Forgiveness is not mine to give.

Acceptance is mine to live.

FRIENDS

Everyone needs
A few old friends
(To remember who they were)
And some new ones
(To accept who they are
becoming)

FULFILLMENT

Be close

But don't cling

Respect is the thing

That keeps a relationship whole.

Be understanding

Not indulgent

New insight will bring

Fulfillment

To your empty bowl.

FREE TO LOVE

I had a child
Who was a part of me.
I had a child.
I gave the heart of me.

I watched my child
Grow apart from me.
I felt my child
Take the heart from me.

But as I watched my child
Growing free from me,
I felt the love returning..
Free to me.

A FRIENDLY SMILE, A TOUCH

IT DOESN'T TAKE MUCH

TO GIVE SOMEONE A LIFT

YOUR THOUGHTFULNESS A GIFT.

THE GREATEST GIFT

THE GIFT IS YOUR HEART

THAT YOU MAY CARE.

THE GIFT IS YOUR TIME

THAT YOU MAY SHARE.

THE GIFT IS YOUR HAND

STRETCHED OUT TO ANOTHER.

THE GIFT IS YOUR LIFE

AS FRIEND AND LOVER.

FOR THE GREATEST GIFT

WE HAVE TO GIVE

IS JUST OURSELVES

AND THE WAY WE LIVE.

ALL IS ONE

IF YOU ARE PART OF ME

AND I AM PART OF YOU

WE CAN NO LONGER BE

THOUGHT OF AS TWO.

WHATEVER IS DONE IS

DONE BY THE ONE

WHO SETS US FREE

WITHOUT BOUNDARY

TO KNOW ALL JOY

UNDER THE SUN.

THE GREATEST GIFT

THE GIFT IS YOUR HEART
THAT YOU MAY CARE.
THE GIFT IS YOUR TIME
THAT YOU MAY SHARE.

THE GIFT IS YOUR HAND
STRETCHED OUT TO ANOTHER.
THE GIFT IS YOUR LIFE
AS FRIEND AND LOVER.

FOR THE GREATEST GIFT
WE HAVE TO GIVE
IS JUST OURSELVES
AND THE WAY WE LIVE.

ALL IS ONE

IF YOU ARE PART OF ME

AND I AM PART OF YOU

WE CAN NO LONGER BE

THOUGHT OF AS TWO.

WHATEVER IS DONE IS

DONE BY THE ONE

WHO SETS US FREE

WITHOUT BOUNDARY

TO KNOW ALL JOY

UNDER THE SUN.

WE ARE ALL MADE OF STAR STUFF
WE AND OUR HEIRS.

WE ARE ALL MADE OF STAR STUFF
SHAPED BY OUR PRAYERS.

TRUTH DOES NOT CHANGE

MERELY OUR PERCEIVING OF IT.

PART III

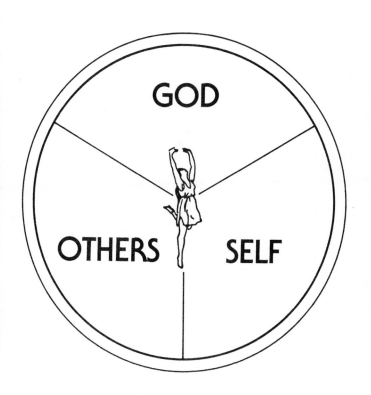

SING AND DANCE

WITH TRUTH

AND CELEBRATE

ALL THAT IS.

GENESIS

NO BEGINNING

WITHOUT END

NO FULFILLMENT

WITHOUT FRIEND

NEVER SUNRISE

WITHOUT SUNSET

NEVER TRUE LOVE

WITHOUT LOVE'S DEBT

NEVER A RAINBOW

WITHOUT RAIN

NEVER GROWING

WITHOUT PAIN

NEVER TIDES

WITHOUT THE SEA

NOTHING ALONE

CAN EVER BE.

REFRACTION

Life is a prism
Reflecting
Souls like a mirror.

Changing as the light
Of Clear Truth
Shines on Discovery
Of new self.

Spreading rainbow hues
Endlessly
As this truth touches
Everyone.

Dividing into
Many truths
All emanating
From one source.

TAKE THE STILLNESS WITH YOU
WHEN YOU WALK INTO THE CROWD.

TAKE THE STILLNESS WITH YOU
TRUE SILENCE SPEAKS OUT LOUD.

TO OTHERS WHO ARE RUSHING
YOU CAN BE A GUIDING LIGHT.

HELPING THEM STOP PUSHING
GIVING THEM NEW INSIGHT.

THE DYNAMIC SILENCE MOVING
CHANGING ALL AROUND
CREATES VIBRATION
LIKE LIVING SOUND.

AUTHOR'S NOTE

My husband and I were driving through the Alps with German friends, when our hosts exclaimed that the snow in the high passes was eternal. It was a haunting phrase which stayed with me. Later that evening in their home, we each shared something personal. Our host played a beautiful violin concerto, and I shared this poem.

The Eternal Snow

The eternal snow
Where Naught can grow
But the chill of approaching
Night.

Where the stillness sleeps
In the stark deep
Of the mountains majestic
Might.

Yet one can see his destiny
Gazing at the wondrous
White.

For we all know
The eternal snow
Reflects the eternal
Light.

JOY

KNOWING NO BOUNDS

ONLY

THE LIMITS OF MY

EXPECTATIONS.

I AM

I am grass and flowers

And birds that sing.

I am snow and wind

And bells that ring.

I am coldest winter

And warmest spring.

My soul is part

Of everything.

And everything is part of me

From tranquil sky to raging sea,

From darkest night to brightest day

all teaching me in some unknown way . .

There is no end to me.

WHY

Why do we insist on death
When life is all around?

Why do we refuse to see
The blessings that abound?

Why can't we accept the truth
That would make us free?

Why can't we KNOW ourselves?
WE ARE ETERNITY.

HOPE

Often lost

Then found

Where least expected

AUTHOR'S NOTE

Poetry is everywhere in our lives. We have only to see in a new way and to listen to our own rhythm. I was sitting in my own backyard when the incredible beauty of the day seemed to embrace me and hold me a gentle prisoner in a moment of time.

INCREDIBLE DAY

Another beautiful day
and my restlessness increases.

I ache to embrace each hour
Hold it tightly in my arms
Savoring each beam of sunlight
Each sweetly sung bird song.

I wish to do so much this day.
But how to justify the use of
Such precious time?

There are books to read
Bulbs to plant
Friends to call
Thoughts to think
Dishes to do and
Beds to make . .

Yet through all
The chaos of my mind
The day intrudes softly saying:
Notice me
Experience me
Sense me
Live me.

and I am reminded of Jesus' admonition:

"I will not be with you always,
Come be with me."
So, I am "being" with the day
Keeping it company as in a death watch
Each moment made more poignant
As the end approaches.

Oh spirit locked within
Longing to be free

To soar above petty views
Of right or wrong

And sing with abandon
Truth's sweet song.

THE JOY OF LIGHT

Stepping out into the sunlight
Warmed my body and
Caused the icy fist within me
To relax and stretch longing
Fingers toward the source.

A momentary cloud passed and
I felt the chill of rejection
Like a door being closed in my
Face.

How vital is the light of life!
The sunlight caresses us and
Wraps us securely in its prisms
Reflecting our joy in being
Accepted.

AUTHOR'S NOTE

Tara Singh is an Indian philosopher who combines eastern and western views and comes to the "STILLNESS". I wrote this poem after attending one of his week-end workshops.

STILLNESS

IN THE STILLNESS

IS A PLACE

WHERE GOD AND MAN

CAN MEET.

WHERE YESTERDAY AND

TOMORROW ARE ONE

WITH THE PRESENT

. . . A RETREAT.

VOICE OF TRUTH

The still small voice of truth

Is deep within us all

Buried by our beliefs

And waiting for the call

Of clarity to set it free

And let us share humanity.

PEACE

Make peace with time
Though you are timeless.

Accept the finite
Though you are infinite.

Pursue the truth
For you are part of it.

SOLITUDE

IN SOLITUDE
MY SOUL ATTUNES
TO AN INFINITE HARMONY.

WHERE GOD'S PRESENCE
FLUTES THE SILENCE
CREATING A SYMPHONY.

I AM GRATEFUL
TO ALL THAT IS
THAT I AM.